YARD

by Kaite O'Reilly

© Kaite O'Reilly 1998

YARD was first performed at the Bush Theatre on 30th September 1998 with the following cast:

Ma	Kate Binchy
Fin	Dawn Bradfield
Da	Peter Dineen
Rory	Aidan McArdle
Skully	Ged McKenna
Director	Julie-Anne Robinson
Designer	Nathalie Gibbs
Lighting Designer	Simon Bennison
Sound Designer	Fergus O'Hare

FOR THE BUSH THEATRE

Artistic Director	Mike Bradwell
General Manager	Deborah Aydon
Literary Manager	Tim Fountain
Production Manager	Tom Albu
Press & Publicity Manager	Alex Gammie
Administrator	David Wright
Assistant Director	Amanda Hill
Stage Managers	Rob Bishop, Zoë Grant, Adrian Pagan
Pearson TV Writer in Residence	Helen Blakeman

The Bush Theatre receives support from London Weekend Television

The Bush Theatre receives support from the Pearson TV TheatreWriters Scheme, administered by Pearson Television and sponsored by The Bill.

ISBN 1 898 736 24 3

This play is fully protected by copyright and any application for public performance or reading should be addressed to Shiel Land Associates, 43 Doughty Street, London WC1N 2LF.

The action takes place in a slaughteryard-knackery in Birmingham over approximately five months.

The first foot, Pork, takes place in the late Summer.

The second foot, Fowl, takes place in the late Autumn.

The third foot, Lamb, takes place in the weeks running up to Christmas.

Three feet make a yard.

The time is the present.

Characters

Da (Bull man Rourke)   Irish immigrant. In his early sixties, a powerful man, well-built after a lifetime of physical work lifting bodies of beef. He is married to Breda.

Ma (Breda Rourke)   Irish immigrant. In her late fifties. Sinewy, but a powerful woman.

Fin (Finoulla Rourke)   Second generation Irish. In her early twenties. Daughter of the Rourkes.

Skully   Irish immigrant. In his mid fifties, a scrawny whippet of a man. The runt of the litter. Brother to the Bull man.

Rory   Probably second generation Irish, or an immigrant from an early age. Fin's contemporary and childhood sweetheart. The Bull man's apprentice.

First Foot

PORK

ACT ONE

Scene One

It is Summer.

A knackeryard. Large plastic abattoir sheets hanging at the back. A meat tree stands up-stage and all the paraphernalia of the cutting room on a well-used butcher's block. The door of a large walk-in cold room is visible. RORY enters whistling, from the shop, a butchering knife in a sheath tied at his waist. At the block, he tries the sharpness of the knife against his thumb. He begins to steel it, ineffectually. He places it with reverence on the block, rearranges the tools until he is satisfied, sighs, then exits.

Several beats. DA enters with RORY, they stand before the butcher's block. DA sharpens knives with great expertise on a steel.

DA   Butchering. It's a skill. Got to keep the tools sharp; have to have them ready, willing, able for the master's hand. Butchering. It's a craft. No, a science, a cartographer, exploring the half-discovered lands. There's always something there not meant to be. I once found a calf with his heart the wrong side. Like mine. Not cut out and glistening, like the others on the tray. Are you paying attention?

RORY   Yes.

DA   It's a magician's act. the sleight of hand. No cock-ups, no thoughts other than the pure steel edge of the knife. One slip up and you're banjaxed - blood on the block and your hand maimed. Sl-ip and you're a seven finger dandy. For what else is our source but a dead form of our fingers, chopping slicing edging tidying as we fillet the beef? Are you paying attention?

RORY   Yes sir.

DA   It's a dying art. All this supermarket crap. Vacuum-packed. Sealed hermetically. Void of a sense of having lived. Plumped to perfection with water injections and dye and additives and god knows what. Where's the sense of mortality gone? The old butcher shop which stank of death - a pig's head in the window, apple artistically gripped in the mouth. That taste of mystery, alchemy, sacrifice. The taint of blood letting, anaemia, sin. A primitive smell. They don't want it anymore, the guilt, the delicious guilt. The Bless me Father for I have sinned. The ten Hail Mary's and a quid in the Mission box before getting slaughtered in the barmaid's arms. They'll have none of that. But they'll eat tofu shaped like a chicken.

MA enters. She looks at them, DA stiffens.

MA   Rory.

RORY   Missus.

MA   Rory, will you tell the Bull man I have a message for him.

A beat. RORY seems confused. MA looks at him. He turns to DA.

RORY   Ah, Bull man, sir, ah... the missus has a message for you.

MA   Will you tell him his great dotey has escaped again..

RORY   His... ?

MA   ... Off, flying down the Stratford Road as we speak, heading for the Bull Ring shopping centre.

RORY   His... ?

MA   Donkey.

DA lets out a roar of anguish and rushes off as RORY tries to relay the message.

RORY   Bull man, your donkey's out and heading for Birmingham...

DA has gone. MA looks at RORY.

RORY   I was just, y'know, passing...

MA looks at him, the knife sheath about his waist, and leaves. RORY removes it, loiters, unsure what to do. FIN appears at the entrance. She speaks to herself.

FIN   Hands up skirts. Always have to have their hands in something.

She enters, dragging a large suitcase. RORY notices her.

RORY   Fin? Jesus, Fin! You're back! It's great to see you, it's... (*He goes to embrace her. She pushes him away. They stand*) You must be tired after the journey. If only you'd let me know you were coming, I would've come and met you.

FIN   It wasn't planned.

RORY   And the Bull man never said you -

FIN — I'm not expected. Pull the gate behind you when you go.

RORY But Fin...

FIN — We don't want the beasts out on the road; more complaints. We're not wanted here as it is.

RORY But...

FIN Visiting time's over, Rory. Haven't you had your fill of the pet lambs?

RORY I'm working here now. The Bull man's given me a job. Not quite official; your Mother doesn't know yet but -

FIN — Is this the best you can do? I'm disappointed, Rory.

RORY I didn't mean to take your place - well, I mean I couldn't, I couldn't now, could I? Take your place, I mean.

FIN There's nothing here for you.

RORY But there's room for both of us - that's if you're back, there is. Room. And I don't need much pay. I just - a little to tide me over, y'know and... I'm a working man, I'm - It's a job - it's a - it's a science.

FIN Are you sure you're not just taking refuge with the rest of the knackers?

RORY The Bull man has a plan for me and... Travel, you know, travelling - it's very tiring and you'll be your old self... in fact you won't know yourself - once you've had a little, a lie down.

FIN There's no future here. Nothing but scavenging and diseased deaths.

RORY Oh, it's not so bad when you get used to it.

MA (*Entering*) Hello, Rory.

RORY Mrs R.

MA Still just passing?

RORY I was.

MA So pass along elsewhere.

RORY I will.

MA   If he does have his dotey back, be careful on the way out. That donkey has a vicious kick.

RORY   But it only has three legs -

MA   Even so. It has a demon left hook. You go careful.

RORY   I will.

He makes to leave, but waits for DA, hidden behind the plastic sheets.

MA   So?

FIN   So, what?

MA   Exactly.

FIN   Ha?

MA   Yes.

FIN   Mother, you're unintelligible.

MA   Oh, so you do know me. You're home, then? So you're back. I'd've killed the fatted calf only they're all anorexic. That or psychotic, geriatric, disabled, maimed. Crawling with lice, ringworm, ticks or a plethora of other parasites, some still unknown to medical science. Your father has a talent for it. Disease-ridden, knackered -

FIN   - I wasn't hungry, anyway.

MA   There's some cheese in the ice-box.

Off, behind sheets, hear DA shouting with the loud wild braying of the donkey.

DA   Fucking cunting bastardising thing. Y'oul hoor, I'll have you.

MA   The donkey.

DA   You knacker. I'll turn you into glue, I will.

MA   He won't part with it.

DA   See how you like being on the back of a stamp. Don't be sneering at me like that, y'bollox. I'll play a tune on your gizzards yet. You'll see and then you'll be smiling the other side of your face. (*Entering*) I'll bloody shoot you.

10

MA   Maybe then we'll all have some peace.

DA   What was that? I thought I heard something.

FIN   Da.

DA   Hush. Now isn't that strange? I could've sworn I heard an angel voice. But och, no. What would the angels be doing down here amongst common men?

MA   Give him the humane killer. Then we'll see if his words count for anything.

FIN picks up the bolt gun.

DA   There it was, again. Finoulla, d'you think I'm having an extasie? D'you think I'm being blessed, having a beatific experience?

MA   Time to confiscate his Lives of the Saints.

DA   (*On knees*) It is! Oh blessed Saint Margaret of the knackeryard! I'm having a vision! The Holy One spoke!

FIN   Daddy -

DA   Hush, now - let me see - I think I can make her out - a beautiful lady with the flowing waxed robes of the slaughterhouse - her hands joined in the holy act of dressing a chicken - the flash of her rubber gloves as she pokes the chicken's arse.

FIN   I'm home.

DA   Shush - and there, see - the symbol of our salvation - Hope - the glistening innards wound as the rosary about her fingers, the rope of intestine and sacrificial blood. Let me but bathe in it and I will be clean, made new, saved - (*MA leaves*) But no, it was the devil tempting. There is no forgiveness. All is murky and corrupt, the grease swimming on the surface of a pail of sick. Why were we put on this earth? To suffer. A big fekking laugh on the behalf of the Almighty. The almighty fek-all. There's nothing.

FIN   Daddy -

DA   (*Seeing humane killer*) Why've you got that?

FIN   For the donkey.

DA   And why would you be wanting to do that? A great little beast it is. The truest friend a man ever had.

FIN   But you just...

DA   There's no explaining love, nor the bond between us and our fellow creatures. Now, put it away. A little girl like you could do a mischief.

She puts the bolt-gun down on the block. With suitcase, she makes to leave into the shop, but sees RORY emerging from his hiding-place. RORY takes his place with DA at the block. They continue as though there was no interruption.

DA   So, Rory my lad. Butchering. D'you think you're ready for it, boy? Can you take the challenge?

RORY   I'm up to it as any.

DA   No, that Gilligan's a wizard when it comes to boning-out. Trained him meself, for all the good it did me. He only went and joined the opposition.

RORY   I'll not do that, sir.

DA   Not unless you want your gullet severed.

RORY   No sir.

DA   That Gilligan... He'll be a fierce opponent, Rory. He can cut round a hipbone so it's gleaming, just the pearly gristle on the ball and socket joint. He's got class. A surgeon's eye. All these farm boys wasting skill on the dead when we should be in Harley street - keyhole operations - steady hands. But because we're from the mick-boat, no fucker'll touch us. Frightened we'll plant semtex when doing a by-pass on a politician's ticker. "Just sew him up, Nurse, and send him to the House of Lords immediately." Ker-boom! Kept off the falling-down water, like I told you?

RORY   Yes.

DA   Show me your hands. Any shaking?

RORY   Steady as a rock.

DA   No tightness, stiffness or loss of co-ordination?

RORY   No, sir.

DA Put them up, put them up! (*They shadow-box*) One, two, one two... Have you been doing the wrist exercises? Show me. You're loose, boy. We may have a chance. But it's work, now... you're in training. No birds booze or punch-ups; we'll have you right and you may have a chance, boy.

FIN appears from her secluded position.

FIN Chance at what?

DA Oh, it's the jezebel calling. You be careful with those ears, girl. Flap, flap - a gust of wind and there's you, kite-ing away.

FIN Chance at what?

DA It's private.

RORY The competition.

DA Y'oul bollox. Hadn't I just said -

FIN Mastercraft butcher? You're putting him in for the Mastercraft Butcher Awards? Jesus, I knew things were bad, but... Daddy, have you gone soft in the head?

DA Finoulla...

FIN He'll be destroyed. He can't even cut meat on his plate, his Mammy has to do it for him.

DA Finoulla...

FIN He doesn't know the sharp side from the blunt. He'll take the hand off himself. Are you wanting to spoil him?

DA Pay no attention to her, Rory boy. You'll be fine.

RORY exits.

FIN And you're even more of an eejit than I thought you to be if you believe that.

DA A Mastercraft Butcher would bring in custom.

FIN You'll be a laughing stock.

They look at each other. Silence. FIN turns to exit.

DA	Finoulla? Child? You were the size of a chicken when I plucked you from your Mother's thighs. I held you, the cord still attached, held you.

(He holds out his hand, palm upwards. She advances, places her hand against his, seeing how far she has grown)

	Don't ever speak to me like that in front of Rory again. He's my apprentice.
FIN	But he's...
DA	... I've worked miracles before, I'll work them again. Do you doubt me?
FIN	No.
DA	A man needs respect. D'you hear?
FIN	Yes, daddy.
DA	Bitch.

He catches her and pulls her to him in a tight embrace.

Scene Two

Large walk-in fridge opens. SKULLY is hanging from an S-hook through his jacket. MA enters.

SKULLY Any chance of a bit of bread and drippin, Ma'am? No?

MA I want never gets.

SKULLY I didn't want any - was just wondering of the chance of it. But surely, in the logic of things, if I want never gets, I don't want - gets?

MA Haven't you enough with the offal?

SKULLY I have lights and sweetbread and all the delicate internal flowerings a man could wish for. But sometimes a man hankers for the usual. Now, a bit of drippin - the lardy stuff with brown jelly - on a hunk of wholemeal bread... now then, I'd be a man at peace with the angels.

MA You're certainly in the position to be communing with them.

SKULLY Oh, that was your Bull; one of his little jokes.

MA At your expense.

SKULLY It's a wise man can laugh without costing himself a penny -

MA - But you've a new suit.

SKULLY I'm the wise man can laugh. This is Bull's best, pilfered from the wardrobe this very morning.

MA He'll have you crucified for it.

SKULLY *(Opening arms, making crucifix)* Isn't that what he's after doing, already? You know the temper with him. If he suspects a precious thing is spoiled, he'll destroy it himself sooner than discover if there's damage or not.

MA That is his way.

SKULLY He was crying before the fibres were broken. Terrible sad at the loss, even before he did the damage. But there you go, no reasoning with him. Will you play Mary Magdalene to my hung Christ?

MA It was his Mother Mary at the pietà.

SKULLY I know my Bible. It's the possibility of the fallen woman I'm talking about. What good would a virgin be to me? You can see yourself, I'm a well-hung man. (*She lifts him down*) Jesus, but you're a mighty woman. Does he have you lifting the bodies of beef?

MA There's more fat on a chip than you.

SKULLY That's the breeding.

MA Ha.

SKULLY Have you ever seen an overweight racehorse? I'm telling you, now, thoroughbreds never get fat.

MA And thieving tinkers never grow old. (*Removes meat from his pocket*) Don't chance your hand with him, Skully.

SKULLY And how about with you?

MA I'm poisoned meat, Skully. Not to your palate.

SKULLY Perhaps it's an acquired taste.

MA Don't.

SKULLY How long has it been, Breda? You and the Bull yoked together? Thirty years? Even the Great Train Robbers got less than that.

MA Finoulla! (*She begins to scrub the block*)

SKULLY And they weren't in solitary confinement.

MA Finoulla! Bring out a basin of hot water.

SKULLY I've never known a pair like you. Living side by side, freezing each other out - but the blood boils beneath the surface...

MA Do you hear me?

FIN (*Entering*) What did your last slave die of?

MA Asphyxiation after I'd pushed her cheeky tongue down her gullet.

FIN I suppose that's better than choking on your own bile.

MA I'll have none of your lip, girl.

FIN   I wouldn't stand so close to her, Uncle Skully. She's like a clump of nettles this morning. She'd sting you.

MA   Mind you don't go cutting yourself on that sharp wit.

FIN   Here's the water. What's old rag and bones doing here?

MA   Kitted himself out in the gentleman's outfitters upstairs and took his fingers for a stroll in the food hall.

FIN   I wouldn't rest your hand on the block if your brother's around.

MA   He had him trussed up like a turkey for Christmas in the cold room when I came down. He'd be there still only the latch slipped the lock.

FIN   Da's losing his touch. He's going soft in his old age.

MA   No, it's the law suit with Gilligan that has him so careless with the door. Three thousand pounds a toe - that's what Gilligan's after. He lost four toes from frost bite when he was left in overnight.

SKULLY   Jesus!

MA   He was asking for it. He broke the rules.

SKULLY   Rules, ballox. I never heard of any -

MA   - There's a code of conduct in this Business, Skully. An internal law... Finoulla?

FIN   You stand firm, you stick with your own and you don't join the other side.

MA   You see? It's not written down, but we all know it.

SKULLY   A man has to try his luck.

MA   Not when the future of the whole business is at risk. We're little fishes Skully, about to be swallowed up by the big supermarket whale. We have to swim together, otherwise there'll be not one of these family knackeries left.

SKULLY   And wouldn't that be a shocking loss to the whole of Western civilization?

MA   You break the rules and you face the consequences. Gilligan knew what he was doing when he went to the other camp. He turn-coated, so he had to be punished.

SKULLY   What is it with yous? Are you all so unforgiving?

MA   It's a matter of survival.

SKULLY   The fella could've lost his foot.

FIN   Well he won't do it again, will he?

SKULLY   Jesus! It's tender this chick should be - not tough like an old broiler.

MA   The world makes them hard soon enough.

SKULLY   And living near the death pen's not going to help much, neither.

FIN   I don't mind it. In fact I quite like it. It has its own charm.

DA and RORY enter. MA immediately exits. DA points out meat in the cold room

DA   Now this was a moo-cow and that a baa-baa black sheep.

SKULLY   What's with the woodentop?

FIN   Da's new apprentice.

SKULLY   Couldn't he get -

FIN   - They're thin on the ground.

DA   Count the ribs

RORY   One, two, three...

DA   Try it in Irish, now. Aon, do, tri...

(SKULLY registers MA has left and leaves quietly, in the same direction. DA brings a shoulder of pork to the butcher's block)

Now with a moo-cow we have top-side, silverside, rump. What else?

FIN   T-bone.

RORY   T-bone, Loin chops, scrag end of neck.

DA   That's sheep, you fekkin mutton-head. Am I wasting my time?

FIN   Da...

DA   If you want to be in with a chance for this competition, you need to know your way around a beast.

RORY Like a cabbie's knowledge?

DA   Just like that, boy. See it as routes around town. Bones are the buildings, the muscles are the roads. Are you ready to orientate yourself?

RORY I am.

DA   So we'll be off. Now: a pork shoulder is detached from the side by cutting and sawing, at right angles to the spine through the fifth vertebra. This removes tissue that belongs to the neck and spine. The bones in the primal cut include the cervical and two thoracic vertebrae -

FIN   - Scapula, humerus and radius/ulna, also known as the knuckle.

DA   The muscles...

RORY Are the main shoulder muscles?

DA   Good lad, plus...? Plus a section of the eye muscle.

FIN   Longissimus dorsi.

RORY Mr R, how come the eye muscle is attached to a pig's shoulder? Doesn't he have them like us, in the usual place?

DA   Jesus Christ! Haven't you seen a bloody pig, Rory?

RORY Not alive.

DA   The eye muscle is connected to the shoulder because that's how the bastard thing grows. Now come on, continue.

RORY I can't. I've never been this far before.

DA   Ah, virgin territory. It's alright, son, your captain has chartered these waters before.

RORY I thought we were on land.

DA   What?

RORY In a taxi.

DA   What the - ?

RORY   The bones were the buildings and muscles the streets. If we've gone to sea, what's -

DA   - I promise you, boy, you'll end up on this block with my knife between your ribs before this competition's done. You'd try the patience of a fucking saint.

RORY   But am I on land or sea? Are you a cabbie or a sea captain?

DA   I'm a fucking butcher, for Christ's sake. I slaughter beasts and believe me, boy, you're fast becoming the next on my list.

FIN   Gently, Da.

DA   Now. At this - crossroads - a meat man has many cutting options.

FIN   One is to remove the knuckle and bone and roll the whole shoulder as one piece.

DA   That's it, girl.

FIN   More commonly, we cut the shoulder in half, the ventral piece containing the knuckle, hand and spring - tough, scraggy but delicious; especially good for braising.

DA   The other is the neck end.

FIN   It is boned, rolled and tied for roasting.

DA   Little marvel she is. Hasn't forgotten what her oul Da taught her, ha?

RORY   Ah, she's great, sir, the best.

DA   So, Rory, my lad, have you got that, now?

RORY   Er...

FIN   Of course.

MA   (*Entering*) Don't forget for the crackling you have to salt and score the skin.

Scene Three

MA is cleaning the blades. FIN is washing the head of the mincer. She washes her hands scrupulously. MA fingers the knives.

MA   Once. Once he could go through me like a knife in soft butter. Warm, sinking, soft.

FIN   They always have to touch.

MA   And the smell of earth. Cooked soil and the sweet white root of grass. The insects crawling but not on me, oh no. Oh my bucking boyo.

FIN   Can't just look. Touch. Have to.

MA   And the whiteness of skin. Dazzling.

FIN   Oil on his hands. Engine oil. Or worse. I'll get an infection.

MA   Tracing the freckles on his shoulders. My knees open to the sun and I saying yes oh yes, my dandy my dangler my -

FIN   What in shite's up with you?

MA   Your bra strap's showing.

FIN   I'm not wearing one.

MA   Well your bubs'll be saying how d'ye do to your navel in no time.

FIN   Cheerful fucker, aren't you?

MA   Your Father taught you language, not me.

RORY enters at a run, a meat cleaver in his back. He collapses onto the stage. MA and FIN approach him. SKULLY enters running, screaming curses from DA following, with the loud braying of the donkey.

SKULLY   Mary Mother in Heaven. He's just after mortally wounding him.

           (RORY groans)

           Jesus, is he still in limb?

MA   It's just his wits have scarpered, not the soul. Come on, Rory boy.

RORY   Have I died and gone to heaven?

SKULLY   Jeez, he must be bad if he thinks that.

RORY   Is it the other place...? Get off, who are you?

FIN   Stop being an eej, it's me.

RORY   Fin? Oh, Fin, I think he got me. Have I got... Is there anything unusual about my back?

FIN   What?

RORY   Is there anything there?

FIN   Shoulder-blades?

RORY   There's nothing else?

FIN   No.

RORY   Are you sure? Look again.

FIN   No, nothing. Nothing at all... Except the meat cleaver sticking half out of your spine.

RORY collapses between them. MA and FIN laugh.

SKULLY   Now look what you're after doing, you vixen.

FIN   It's the old hatchet in the back joke.

         (*She removes the cleaver and coat as one, the cleaver stuck into a lump of meat between the shoulders*)

FIN   We always play it on the new boys in the front of shop. "Here, try this on; you're a butcher boy, now." Da pretends to pick a fight and... (*mimes thumping in the back*)

MA   Are you back with us, Rory boy?

SKULLY   Yous're all sick, bad as each other. My heart ... it's not strong - I'm not able for yous.

RORY groans.

MA   Are you back? Welcome. You're one of the family, now.

FIN   You've been initiated.

MA   You're one of us.

SKULLY Jesus, who'd be wanting to? You're all mad.

DA enters on a roar, clutching a blood-stained knife.

DA   Where is he? Where's the little runt? I'll cleave him in two, I will. I'll make mincemeat of him to sell to his Mammy.

        (RORY panics, goes to run. All but SKULLY laugh)

        Did you see his face?

MA   And the way he went down between us like a stunned beast.

DA   Aw, come here, now, Rory boy.

RORY   You can piss off; I'll have none more of you.

DA   Come to Daddy; all's forgiven.

FIN   I told you he'd get his own back for telling the customers what's in the cheap sausages.

DA   It's the training I'm giving him. I tell you, a little knowledge is a dangerous thing.

FIN   *('Doing' Rory)* "A pound of sausages, Madam? Let me tell you, it's alchemy, magic. In this we have the heart of a lamb, the guts of a sheep, the lungs from a cow... held together with the membrane of a pig's intestine. Now, if you didn't know better, you'd never guess that, would you?"

DA   And out of the shop she was with a threat to report us to Health and Safety. You'll not do that again, will you? Will you?

RORY   No. No I won't because I quit.

DA   And run off like Gilligan did, with all that training to the Competitors?

RORY   I wouldn't do a thing like that.

DA   I warned you what would happen if you did, boy.

SKULLY Ignore him, lad. You stand your ground.

SKULLY runs as DA turns to him.

RORY   That wouldn't be right. I wouldn't, I wouldn't, I -

FIN   He's loyal.

DA   He's one of us. So you won't be chatting up the customers in the front of shop now, will you, son? Giving away our trade secrets, ha?

RORY   I didn't know them things weren't supposed to be put into the sausages. The waste, she called it, the rubbish.

DA   And what's wrong with it, anyway? Aren't we just being modern, being green? They're all very keen to recycle their newspapers and wine bottles - isn't the meat business the most ecological of them all? Not a scrap is wasted - not even the hooves. They go onto the flap of an envelope they lick most every day.

FIN   You'd be turning them all vegetarian.

DA   Aw, get out of here with that. They're in uproar about some knacker pony but they'd step over you if you fell down in the street. Wouldn't give you the drip off the end of their nose - but if it has four legs, they'd fucking marry it.

MA   And probably get better mileage than a two legged animal.

DA   I must be saying me prayers right; the saints are out today.

MA   I'd say a four legged pig'd be more kindly than the biped variety. It's a bad breed. Cut you soon as look at you.

DA   Quick, Finoulla, call the priest. The Moving Statue's getting very chatty and I'd like the miracle to be verified.

SKULLY Have you no sense at all between yous?

DA   And there's the fallen Seraphim come to the Blessed Margaret's aid.

SKULLY Why d'you have her named after a saint?

MA   Because he does have me martyred.

DA   She martyrs herself, every living day. She hasn't mastered the last nail through the palm into the wall, yet, but I'm expecting it any moment. She rejoices in her suffering and does extra penance. If you hang around a bit, she might do some mortification of the flesh. She loves an audience.

MA   Ah, yes, the bruises got there by themselves, would you believe? The

	scars splitting my forehead and lacerating the once smooth skin. Ah, yes, it's truly miraculous, or is y'man there saying I'd do that on purpose, to spite my flesh?
DA	She'd do anything to spite me. It's in her nature. Tormented me from the moment I saw her. Thought I couldn't fucking live without her and now I know I can't fucking live with her. And she'll be there, the thorn in my side, the barbed belt in my flesh until the day comes one of us kills the other.
MA	Finoulla, go to your room.
FIN	I'm not ten anymore.
MA	Finoulla go to your room and bring out your babby diary.
FIN	My -?
MA	Get the book.
FIN	That's private -
MA	Alright, I know it by heart. "17th October: Crunch went Mammy's bone when daddy punched her in the face."
SKULLY	Breda..
MA	"20th October: Mammy crying again..."
SKULLY	There's no cause for this.
MA	"15th November: Mammy back from hospital with her hand in a sling."
SKULLY	Stop it now.
MA	Finoulla, what does your father think of your diary as a nine year old? Ha? (*A beat*) Skully, your precious brother has fallen terrible silent all of a sudden. I wonder, has he lost that great tongue of his? Or is it shame?
	(*The silence continues to fall*)
	I said: would it be shame?
RORY	I'll go and see if there's any customers, shall I? I mean, with us jabbering here, they could be out of the shop with joint, till and all... So I'll... shall I? (*He leaves*)

MA continues to out-stare DA. He shuffles off.

MA Typical. Same as between the sheets. He'd come in roaring like a lion and go out like a lamb. Finoulla, remember to tell your Father to be more particular in his buying. That lamb turned out to be mutton and the heifers were all in calf. We can't keep running this business as a charity for any scrag-end no other body'll touch. The same applies to the tinker. I want him gone.

She leaves in silence.

SKULLY We had a cockerel once, at home. Gad, it was full of itself. King of the shit pile, where he'd strut and crow and fly at you, spurs sparking, soon as glance at you. The fights he and the Bull had! Always turkeycockin'. One day the cock flew at your da and him bending over, digging the spuds - got him full-force on the arse - and the screams! The blood was up in the Bull and he chased the fekker with his shovel until - bang! - he hit it on the crown with the full tilt of the spade. The cockerel lay there - stunned - maybe dead. Didn't we all come running out and find the eejit cradling the fowl and trying to blow into its beak? The kiss of life, it was. That's how it's always been with him. He was sorry once he destroyed it.

FIN What happened?

SKULLY We had the cock in a little stew with the taytees. There were tears in his eyes as he ate - savouring the character more than the meat. There's nothing like knowing the personality of your grub to add poignance to the sauce. God, he loved that bird. So I'll be off.

FIN Don't be straying too far.

SKULLY leaves as RORY enters. FIN presses RORY to the floor and lies beside him. He covers them both with the plastic tarpaulin of the slaughterhouse.

Scene Four

MA   First you dismember. Then you remember. Lying back in the sweet green grass of home. The flesh goosepimpling; drying off in the sun. Naked, we were, but at ease and the laughter of it, the joy of it, a smile ready on the mouth. And me laughing. Oh yes, my lad, my lackey, my dandy dandler. I love you, I will my love, my darlin, my own. I loved you, you... I gave you my all.

MA leaves. FIN sits up from beneath the tarpaulin. RORY wakes also.

RORY   Fin? Oh, Fin..

FIN rises, puts away the plastic sheeting.

FIN   Another alternative when dealing with a shoulder of pork is to take the neck end, bone and roll it, then tie for roasting.

RORY   Fin?

He approaches, tries to be tender, she moves away.

FIN   Each butcher has their own method when handling shoulder of pork.

RORY   Listen...

FIN   We favour the traditional 'blade-bone' roasting joint, which is virtually archaic, now.

RORY   I -

FIN   So if you're going for the Mastercraft butcher awards you'll need to know these things.

(DA enters, sighing heavily, without his usual swagger. He sighs, waits, then sighs again)

That's a terrible big sigh. *(RORY exits)* You'll wear out your lungs at that rate.

DA   I've worn every other fucker else. It's a wonder I'm still walking. A bag of bones, a suit of skin. We should put up a sign on the gate and charge admission: 'Come and see the miraculous breathing corpse. No pulse, no heartbeat, but the lights keep inflating.'

FIN   Don't be so maudlin.

DA Or maybe we could invite the neighbours to come and have a dig at me. Everybody else is. I can't open me mouth without one of yous jumping down me throat. What is it, 'have a go at Rourke day'? Are the scouts selling flags?

FIN Now you're being silly.

DA Finoulla, if you haven't a word of kindness for me, I'd rather you didn't speak at all.

FIN You never hear what I say anyway.

DA Exactly. Just - go and help your Mother and take her side as you always do. Don't worry about me. I'm fine. Better on my own. Maybe that way I'll be happy.

FIN Daddy -

DA Just - leave me alone.

FIN You don't really want me to.

DA So after taking my heart and breaking my spirit, you want my head, too? What are you: fucking mind-readers?

FIN You're not being fair.

DA Fair? What's fair? If life was fair I wouldn't be living out the end of my days in this fucking tip. Bull the meat man. Rourke the slaughterman. It's tainted me. I can't get the smell off. She hated it. Would see her nose curling up every time she got a whiff of me, trying to be close. Aw, it was fine when I was a farmboy - honest sweat, the sweet smell of hay. But now I'm corrupted. And so is she. And I'm glad. I'd dance for it. Her with the lily white hands - so cool they were - like touching an angel. Delving amongst the cancers now they are. Touching things that shouldn't be touched. Knowing things. "So that's what a disease looks like." She said it the first time I showed her. "Cancer. My Father died of that." And all the time wondering if they're growing in you. That death. From a single cell. That simple death.

FIN embraces DA. MA enters.

MA Finoulla, when you've finished comforting the dying, I want a hand cleaning the blocks.

DA Is it any wonder I'm the walking fucking wounded? I'm eaten alive by that deadly fucking tapeworm coiled up inside me. I can't get rid of her.

Maybe if I slit my belly I could pull her out but what would be left? She's eaten the insides out of me.

MA   And when the sob-story's over, maybe you'll earn your keep, girl?

DA   Oh Finoulla, what's become of us? I'm mad. I've gone mad. I'm going mad.

DA exits in distress. FIN tries to comfort, to follow, but is shrugged off.

FIN   Why did you do that? You've already won today but no, that's not enough, you have to come in and gloat, to stir up the shit.

MA   I see you've been taken in by his amateur dramatics. He should've got a job with the Abbey players but he couldn't bear to leave his pigs.

FIN   I never want to be like you.

FIN begins to leave.

MA   He had me conned. Along the coast of Bray and him sweeping his hand across all we saw. "Do you want it?" he asked "It's yours". I believed him. He could scrape it all into a handkerchief and throw it to the stars. And what did I get?

A beat.

FIN   Mammy. You never asked me why I'd come back.

MA   You never volunteered.

FIN   I think I'm pregnant.

MA   Well, you'll be at home amongst the donkey and the beasts, then.

FIN   It was no virgin conception.

MA   They never are.

FIN   There wasn't even love.

MA   More fool you.

FIN   Mammy, why are you so hard on me?

MA   Because otherwise I'd break. Now get the steel brush to help me with these blocks.

Second Foot

FOWL

ACT TWO

Scene One

Time has passed. It is Autumn. RORY enters, calling and looking for FIN, his hands cupped protectively before him. A sense of excitement.

RORY   Fin! Fin? Look what - Fin... Look - Myrtle made it! Fin? I've got something for you!

SKULLY   *(Appearing, very dapper)* You shouldn't cup your heart so in your hands. The lassies like to think a boy chases a girl until she catches him.

RORY   Skully!

SKULLY   The very article.

RORY   You're back!

SKULLY   Steady, now lad. I haven't been away that long. *(Refers to RORY's hands)* What's the cod piece?

RORY   It's Myrtle. She's laid her first egg.

SKULLY   And there's us all thinking she was shell-shocked and unable.

RORY   I told you all she needed was a little time and understanding.

SKULLY   I suppose you were on the nest with her, Dr Doolittle, urging her on? Have you made any progress with the donkey?

RORY   He doesn't kick or bite me anymore.

SKULLY   Probably eternally grateful for the wooden leg you fashioned for him from the old banister. Have you practiced your dentistry yet? Removed his teeth? I suppose he could still gum a fella to death.

RORY   What?

SKULLY   Nothing, son. Just having my fun. What's happening in this old morgue? Not a sight or sound of welcome and me the prodigal, returned from the big city. It's that cold and lonesome it'd put a shiver down the spine of a year old corpse. Where is everyone, son?

RORY   The Bull man's in washing-up after the slaughter. It must've been good killing, he's whistling.

SKULLY Either that or his conscience is pricking and he's cheering up his spirit. It gets him like that sometimes. He wanted to grow the blasted things, not slay them. One thing you can be sure of, if the Bull's grinning and in high form, his soul's in mortal combat in hell. If it isn't that, he's getting more silence from the missus. On the other hand, he could be just cheerful.

RORY That's more than one thing.

SKULLY I never claimed to be a numerate man.

Hear DA, off, with the loud braying of the donkey.

DA That's it, my sweetheart, my sugar; I'll put a lump of metal in your brain one day and then you'll be sorry. (*He enters*) Skully! Are you back with us?

SKULLY No, this is but my walking shadow. My spirit has quitted the body, for the living can haunt as soon as the dead. My spirit has broken the thread, travelling here, whilst my body lies elsewhere.

RORY Where, Skully?

SKULLY Besides a well-heeled widow in a penthouse in Knightsbridge.

DA You're her rough rider, then?

SKULLY A woman like that recognizes class. She saw I had no dirt under my fingernails, so I was a gentleman at heart.

DA Lazy devil by vocation. I've never known a skiver like you.

SKULLY Don't be showing your jealousy, Bull. As for skiving, I never sweated so much in my toil even when I was a hod carrier.

DA He lasted a day.

SKULLY I have vertigo. Couldn't stand the heights.

DA That was his alibi for a little cat burglary he was being investigated for.

SKULLY Could you see me scaling a drainpipe?

DA I've seen you slithering down one when the husband come home.

SKULLY Whist, protect the innocent.

DA So the merry widow's fella was your size, then? Them are damn fine feathers.

SKULLY Which make the fine bird and you know what they do, flock together. Soirees in Knightsbridge, Rory; a box at the Opera - she might like me in my civvies in the bedroom, but outside I was strictly incognito. The Viscount of the last out-post of the Empire - a brave little settlement standing firm against the twentieth century and its fal-de-la nonsense. A place where slavery is embraced and the white memsahib can sleep easy at nights...

RORY In India?

SKULLY In County Cork, where the red jackets still ride to hounds and men's suits have plackets for easy access. Ah, the Viscount of K-cuf eht hsilgne, as it is known in our native tongue.

DA Or fuck the english, if you're not reading from left to right.

SKULLY Oh, the butcher's slang for me! I never knew I'd miss it so much, Llub!

DA Ah, it's a dying language. Eht gnuoy seno t'nod wonk ti reomyna.

SKULLY A truer word you never said.

RORY What?

SKULLY (*Translating*) The young ones don't know it anymore.

RORY Is it Latin?

DA What chance do we have to survive when they've all but stamped out the mother tongue?

RORY Teach me, then.

DA Dangerous waters, son. An all but illegal act. They forbade us to use it; said it was the tongue of treachery, of conniving and cunning. Laws there were made against it. No language but Queen's English in the shop.

SKULLY If a man can't be king of his own quarter, well, he may as well give up now. No language, no culture.

DA No culture, no future. Sad days, Skully, sad days. Eht feeb sisirc and stekramrepus evah su lla netae pu.

RORY What?

SKULLY (*Translating*) The beef crisis and supermarkets have us all eaten up.

DA There is but one family abattoir in the whole of the city, and we're standing in it. We're the last of the Mohicans, the end of the true tribe.

SKULLY Ah, no, Bull.

DA Old Kavanagh's butcher shop closed last week. It's been on the same spot on the Coventry Road for thirty years and - Bam! ... gone. The landmarks are changing, Skully. And the cattle market, where you'd once have had a bit of craic, it's like the grave. All the beef farmers are turning the twelve-bore inwards. Fucked.

SKULLY It's never that bad.

DA We're held to siege! Every roundabout has a hyper-market growing off it. There's a new by-pass being built to take the traffic off this road. By-pass to Shopper's Haven ... an operation which'll still this heart, not save it. And what chance do we have? They're even laying on buses to take the shoppers to the complex.

SKULLY Aw, now, Bull, there's got to be a way... there has to be a scam.

DA The competition. That's my final hope. Mastercraft Butcher of the Year from the sole independent abattoir in the Midlands...

SKULLY Are you entering it yourself?

DA How can I now? It's for the newcomers.

He gestures at RORY. A beat.

SKULLY Can't you put the girl in? She's fair handy with a knife.

RORY Sorry, but it's for... it's for the men only, sir.

SKULLY So it's dolly dreamer, then? I see I've come just at the right time. Now, Bull, I met a very interesting fella on my travels. Educated, a gentleman and scholar. He put a proposition to me which I wouldn't mind pushing your way.

DA What is it?

SKULLY D'you know Darwin's theory of evolution, Rory? We were fish, spawned in the sea, crawled out and climbed trees.

DA Aw, for fuck's sake -

SKULLY - We adapted Bull, grew hardy, grew lungs instead of fins. We changed in the face of our environment.

RORY Are you suggesting we go back to the sea?

SKULLY No, lad, that'd be suicide. 75% of all fish is bought frozen. The supermarkets already cater for that - we want something that they don't supply, but for which there's a steady demand. Tell me now, should the ice age come - should the temperature fall below a certain level, we would all perish, is that right?

RORY Below a certain level, yessir.

SKULLY Man, beast, fish, fowl - all would perish?

RORY Yessir.

SKULLY No sir. One living thing would continue. A creature which lives in the highest places in Britain. A creature so rare it cannot be raised in captivity.

DA What is it, man?

RORY A yeti?

SKULLY The Grouse, my friends - Capercaille. And that little creature's going to save our skins.

RORY In the Ice Age?

SKULLY What other age do we live in? I have quitted my merry widow's bed like Moses coming down the mountain. I have come to show you the way. The future, my friends, doesn't lie in some bollox of a competition, nor in trying to sell cheap beef no fucker'll touch. Like Saul on the road to Damascus I have seen the light. Our future is in catering for the quality ... duck, goose, grouse - the future is Game. And I know just the man who'll give us a good deal.

Scene Two

FIN scrubs the block. She is just perceptibly pregnant. RORY enters, carrying knives. A bloody rag is wrapped around a finger.

RORY   Oval knife, straight knife, boning knife and cleaver.

FIN   Don't be seen at the front of shop with that rag on your finger. Health and Safety'd be down on us like a ton of bricks. The customers wouldn't like it, either - them we've managed to keep.

RORY   Business'll pick up. I used the tail grab wrong.

FIN   That'll teach you to use the tools properly.

RORY   I slipped - I didn't know... I skinned me finger.

FIN   Fifty cuts make a butcher.

RORY   (*He points*) The first scar from the boning knife. And I have Fin, you know - a constant ring in me ear from when the Bull man hit me after watching me cut myself. He said I wouldn't make that mistake again.

FIN   And will you?

RORY   No.

FIN   So it works then.

RORY   He says I'm improving, which isn't bad considering the divil of a job he has grooming me. He says, he says that great butchers are born, not made... But seeing he hasn't got one of them, I'll have to do.

(FIN goes to lift a bread tray of cuts to bring to the cold room)

RORY   Here, I'll do that.

FIN   I've been lifting bread trays since I was ten years old.

RORY   I know, but -

FIN   To be fit you ought to be able to lift your own weight and near jump your own height. Did you know that?

RORY   The Bull man told me this morning.

FIN   Well I can take a hundred weight and this is no bother.

RORY   Yes, but

FIN   What?

RORY   Well...

FIN   What?

RORY   Ought you be - lifting things I mean?

FIN   It's hardly going to sprout legs and walk to the cold room by itself.

RORY   No, I mean...

FIN   What?

RORY   I'll do it for you. Let me. Let me do the picking and carrying for you.

FIN   And let me go soft? You've got to be hard, Rory, or people will take advantage. You better toughen up.

(She lifts the load and carries it to the cold room. RORY follows. As she turns RORY is facing her, very close. They look at each other)

Do you want something?

RORY   No. I'm fine, thanks.

FIN   Are you sure?

RORY   Yes.

FIN   Then leave off being my shadow.

(She moves away, busying herself at the block. He stands)

And stop looking at me. I can't think with you bloody looking at me.

RORY leaves. FIN tidies the block. DA enters from the shop, in a barely controlled rage. He looks at FIN, a sense of him recognizing her pregnancy. She stands.

DA   Finoulla. *(A roar)* Finoulla!

FIN   *(She turns to him)* Yes, daddy.

Blackout.

Scene Three

MA putting hearts on a tray. SKULLY enters.

MA The fly-by-night's looking very hoighty-toighty.

SKULLY A gilded tongue can unlock even the rustiest gate. All you need is a little oiling.

MA I think I prefer it dry, thanks.

SKULLY You need a little spring in your desert. An oasis of clemency.

MA Your time as a lady's fancyman's not improved your poetry. I'd say it's got worse.

SKULLY It's not good for you, Breda. You've become parched.

MA And you're parchment. I can see right through you. Cheap pheasants. Not so cheap after you've had your cut.

SKULLY Breda, you've gone that dry you're brittle.

MA What's the profit you're making off our backs?

SKULLY A woman should be rounded, full of juice.

MA I see I'll get no sense from you.

SKULLY Succulent you should be, like a poached pigeon breast.

MA Or a woodcock, roasted whole on a slice of bread? You'll not spoon out my entrails; you won't have my heart on a plate.

SKULLY You know you have mine.

MA I sent it back; I found it false.

SKULLY The sacred organ has two chambers - although separate, they beat as one. Can we not be the same? Beat together, though we keep our separate rooms?

MA I'd like to see you get in past the donkey. Your brother has it trained better than a watchdog. And what is salvaged from the hooves will be set upon by the gander.

SKULLY He protects his own.

MA   He does in me tail. He turns them wicked as he does all living things. If it has no spirit, he'll destroy it and when there is spirit, it turns bad. He wouldn't know how to treat a creature kindly even if we came with instructions.

SKULLY So why do you stay with him?

MA   I don't. I stay against.

SKULLY That's a terrible sad way to spend your life.

MA   It'll do for me.

SKULLY But isn't it a waste?

MA   I'm no good for anything else.

SKULLY Jesus, Breda, why don't you leave?

MA   This is my home. Not much, perhaps, to you, but it's all I have.

SKULLY Breda -

MA   - It's mine.

SKULLY But -

MA   - No. And don't forget, I'm watching you.

DA enters, carrying a hare. He calls off, to RORY.

DA   Get the others in, boy; we'll have a little lesson.

        (RORY enters, with more bloodied rags on his hands)

        I'll teach you how to skin one so it's off in one piece. Sell it to the rich bastards at eastertime - proper bunny costumes for their little babby darlins. Or perhaps we could stuff them and sell them to your fancy pals in Knightsbridge, ha, Skully? Added authentic decoration for hanging over their Aga with the wicker baskets and dried flowers? Unsheath your knife, Lad.

RORY   I'm not touching that after myxomatosis.

DA   Rabbit's for the peasants. It's hare we're looking at - the bold captain of the fields - and worth three times its poor cousin. The long ears up, tips of fur above the grass. And boxing, boy! Did you ever see a hare fight?

RORY   That's rabbit.

DA   It's hare, boy! See by its athlete legs and its little fists up, ready for the combat.

RORY   Dead. It's a dead rabbit.

DA   Hare! Never was there such a one for courtship.

RORY   We had one called Flossie. It'd be like eating a relative.

DA   With the wooing and the courting and the fighting. Real romance. The better buck winning the doe. Its nature gone wild itself.

RORY   So why did you kill it?

DA   Well, I didn't. I got it from the market.

RORY   You shouldn't encourage them, then, if you think it's so romantic. Poor little Flossie.

DA   Jesus fucking Christ and all the saints in heaven! Whoever heard of a butcher boy gone maudlin over game?

RORY   It's only little. It's not a fair contest.

DA   D'you think it ever was? It's not High Noon. A beast and I don't fight a duel - may the best mammal win. I think you're losing your brains, boy.

SKULLY   Like the mad march hare, swooning in love.

DA   Love? In lust, more like. That's the truer emotion and it doesn't last. There'll be time for the skirts, for the lrigs once the competition's done. They'll be swarming over you like flies over shit if you win.

SKULLY   Always one with a romantic turn of phrase.

DA   So take out your weapon, boy.

RORY leaves.

MA   He's sulking because he saw the birds.

SKULLY   No, he's upset about what happened to Finoulla.

DA starts skinning the hare.

MA   Finoulla? What?!

SKULLY   Aw, nothing. She's fine. Isn't she there cleaning the offal in the gut room?

MA   That's your job.

SKULLY   Bull and me were thinking to put my talents elsewhere. After all, I'm the brains of this business, let her be the guts.

DA   It's a job with dignity, like any other.

SKULLY   Besides, it does make me retch. I haven't got the stomach for it.

MA   And you think she has?

SKULLY   She's throwing up anyway with the unfortunate condition she's got herself into. And she can't be seen in the front of shop, not like that. It wouldn't be decent.

MA   So putting her away with the aborted calves, is?

SKULLY   Ah, she's fine, hardy, not a bother on her. The image of you two, not letting an oul bruise get in the way of business.

MA   Bruise?

SKULLY   It's nothing..

MA   She's bruised? How?

SKULLY   From that little tumble down the stairs.

MA   Mother of God!

SKULLY   Don't flap, she's fine.

MA   When?

SKULLY   A little earlier there, when I come in. The Bull man was helping her up from a little knot on the floor.

MA   The Bull...? The Bull. (*MA realizes. She faces DA*) You pushed her.

DA   She spoke to me!

MA   You...

DA   Fucking Jesus, I'm not hallucinating, she did speak!

MA   You can't get at me anymore, so you use her.

DA   She did! After... how many years? Five? Ten?

MA   Is there nothing you won't stoop to to get that knife in my ribs?

DA   She did!

MA   And your own daughter...

DA   (*Laughing*) She's talking to me, Skully!

MA   My daughter... I curse you.

DA   We're tied together.

MA   I curse you. (*She exits*)

DA   You curse me, you curse yourself.

               (*DA puts his knife down. He turns to SKULLY*)

               And what are you gawping at?

Scene Four

FIN speaks as she changes from overall and striped apron of front of shop to the white gown and rubber boots of the gut room. She moves cautiously, aware of her body's fragility.

FIN   I remember walking the fields with my Father. I was tiny. Fronds of wet grass sticking to my feet. It was early. A Sunday morning. We were picking mushrooms. He could see them from fifty paces and him bending, plucking them from the soil, so tender. He said "Why do I need to go to mass when walking these fields is prayer enough? God is here, not in some fekking building."

And yet I heard her bone crack when he slammed the door on her arm that night. And her legs fell away from under her ... but she didn't make a sound. Not a cry. And that way she wins.

The transformation is complete. She prepares. RORY enters.

RORY   Woodcock. Snipe. Plover. Quail.

FIN   The only birds left in Italy, they say, are in Vatican Square.

RORY   Mallard. Teal.

FIN   Pigeons: dirty rats with wings. They'll eat anything, including each other. Flying vermin.

RORY   Grey legged Partridge.

FIN   I'm going to run the guts. Do you want to help?

RORY   Capercaillie. Grouse.

FIN   I'm the gutman, now. Gutman. They've never heard of equal opportunities.

RORY   Becasse. Becassine.

FIN   Though who wants the opportunity of washing the shit out of the third intestine of a corpse is beyond me. Still, it's survival.

RORY   Becassine.

FIN   Snipe, Rory, Snipe. The quality aren't going to be of such a quality you have to speak French with them.

RORY   Becassine.

FIN You have a point. I've noticed people buy a lot of tripe when it's retitled 'Farthing' - or, even better, 'The Book'. Appeals to their middle-class aspirations, I suppose. "Look, Madam, it's spherical, with one layer of skin closely packed upon another - like pages - like the leaves of a book. Hence we use the ancient folkterm; and how literary of you to eat such a thing..." What you don't know, Madam, is I've had to wash between every single leaf to ensure no shit remains, like an unwanted bookmark, a corner turned down in what was once an animal's digestive system. What you don't know is, to make these sausages and black puddings, I've had to remove intestines, open them and wash them out. With the intestine, it's rather like attaching a garden hose to a running tap - and the faeces...

RORY ... Stop it.

FIN You were listening.

RORY I can't stand it.

FIN Tough. The faeces and muck -

RORY Stop it. (*He tries to hold her*)

FIN Let go - are washed away into the drains. Meanwhile, whilst making black pudding

RORY Stop, Fin.

RORY, with gentleness, tries to hold FIN and silence her.

FIN The gutman, ie me, stirs blood in a big pot - Let go of me -

RORY I can't, no -

FIN - stirring the blood continuously to ensure it doesn't thicken.

RORY Becassine or the snipe, Fin

FIN And I stir it as it cools

RORY Do you know where it comes from?

FIN And as it cools, I take out what looks like sponge

RORY Do you know?

FIN And then I mix the unclotted blood with diced fat, pearl barley and seasoning

RORY From Scandinavia.

FIN Then I run them into beef or pig gut, tying in twists

RORY The Becassine flies from Scandinavia, Fin.

FIN and blanch them in boiling water.

RORY Fin?

FIN When they rise to the top - that is, when the blood cooks, I know they're ready to bring into the shop.

RORY Becassine. Snipe. She flies from Scandinavia.

FIN For white pudding, I add lungs.

RORY The Snipe flies from Scandinavia. Fin, Fin. Snipe.

FIN Snipe?

RORY From Scandinavia. Our little Snipe, it flies from Scandinavia.

FIN Scandinavia?

RORY Yes! And you thought she was local. The Snipe-Becassine flies from Scandinavia at the first full moon in October, beating her path down from the Lake District to the border of England and Wales. That's her flight path, over Lake Conniston, turning right over the trees, heading down to Offa's Dyke and the Bordercountry. Think of her flight! Her freedom!

FIN But she's still caught.

RORY Not always.

FIN There's a dozen in the coldroom, Rory. Go look. She's caught and I am the gutman.

Third Foot

LAMB

ACT THREE

Scene One

MA and DA are at the front of shop, serving customers. Italics signify speech to customer.

MA   You're nothing. You have nothing. All you have are the dirty balls between your legs. *And half a pound of rashers. Is that streaky or back bacon?*

DA   Ah, beloved wife. I should've taken the bolt gun to you on our honeymoon night.

MA   I wish you had. *Streaky.* I'd've been saved this suffering. But why didn't you finish me off when you had the chance? You didn't have the guts. *Thank you.*

DA   A stun gun's too humane. *And how about our special offer - a new departure in our butchering. A brace of lovely, succulent woodcocks. Surprise your old man this evening, and he may surprise you tonight!* I wouldn't waste the bolt on you. *So tender they are and so well-hung. The necks are ready to melt off the hook. Just imagine that in your mouth!*

MA   *I don't blame you, I'm not that keen on game, either.*

DA   *But nothing ventured, nothing gained. You never know until you try it!*

MA   *Okay, love.*

DA   *I'll give you a special price!*

MA   *Bye.*

DA   *And how about you, Madam?* At least with a beast you know it's alive. *Fancy a change, a break out into the unknown, the untasted? No? Come on, be adventurous!* You've never been human. *Christmas is coming...*

MA   *Best mince or cheap mince? Bone-ends? I never knew you had a dog. Stray? You don't want to waste money on good meat for someone else's dog, no.*

DA   You're cast in stone.

MA   Because I've been petrified by you. *Boil the bones up and you'll get a*

	good soup from it - just what hubby'll need in from the Christmas shopping.
DA	*You don't want frozen turkey for Christmas dinner! How about a goose - or, extra special, some grouse? I could do you a very good deal...*
MA	*It may seem expensive, but it's actually less than we paid for it.*
DA	*Yes, this is a cut-throat business, ha ha, but we're actually cutting our own throats to offer this price. No? Well, fuck off, then. Ha ha, my joke. Season of good will, and all...*
MA	*It's at the turning, off the new by-pass.*
DA	*What you don't understand is, they don't grow on trees, just sit on them, ha ha.*
MA	*You can't miss it.*
DA	*See you again? Have a good Christmas.*
MA	*It's sign-posted. Shoppers Haven.*
DA	*Hope you choke on a frozen chicken bone and your children get salmonella and die...*
MA	*Bye.*
DA	Alabaster Saint.
MA	Don't start; I'm not listening.
DA	I would look at you with your cast-down eyes and wonder at the warmth of you;
MA	I don't want this.
DA	- that sweet sourness of your mouth's taste -
MA	I'm going on my break.
DA	You can't - that shiver of the body-warmed medal of the Virgin Mary you wore against your throat.
MA	No.
DA	That a chain could be so warmed by you and still be metal.

48

MA   I'm going on my break.

DA   I thought it would be molten, molten gold rivering your neck.

MA   Brass, or coloured tin. Not gold. Even then your presents weren't real. It stained me, a collar of mould. I should've seen it then as a sign. He will yoke you and you'll be branded, bruised by his husbandry.

DA   I never locked you up.

MA   You locked me out. Out of the warmth and the fire and the old age I thought I'd share with you. You closed the door on me the first time your fist sent me across the room.

DA   I was provoked.

MA   I'm getting old. My skin is crepe at the throat. I look like your rotting turkey gizzards.

DA   Breda -

MA   Don't use my name. There is power in calling a name. You relinquished that when your words cut the heart out of me.

DA   I want to talk to you.

MA   It's past the time for talk. I don't even want to look at you.

DA   Breda...

MA   I want my break.

DA   Surely we can talk?

MA   Rory! Skully!

DA   Can't we patch up our differences?

MA   Just leave me alone.

DA   I'm doing my best to make it all right - in the front of the fuckin' shop when any fekker could walk in -

MA   Rory!

DA   - and me here, a fekkin omathon, pleading with her for a little gentleness -

MA   I can't bear it.

DA — a little calm going into our old age

MA Haven't you tormented me enough?

RORY (*Entering*) What's the missus in a lather about?

DA I'm here trying to reconcile, standing like a fuckin' fool with my heart in my hand

MA You bastard.

DA And that's what I get. You heard it yourself, Rory - as sure as God and you are my witness...

MA Why don't you just go?

DA See? She doesn't want her cake and eat it; she wants the whole fuckin' bakery.

MA Give me some peace.

DA And it's my business. And she wants me to leave. Thirty years I've spent, building this up -

MA On my dowry.

DA Just so she can chase the customers away when things're looking good.

MA We're ruined.

DA A new venture, being the entrepreneurs -

MA The business is destroyed -

DA - Breaking into a new market, attracting new custom -

MA All they want is the cheapest off-cuts. They'd buy the meat we scraped off the block if they thought it'd save them a penny.

DA And she's there, the saboteur -

MA They don't want game!

DA - not just killing the business, but the dream! She has us ruined, Rory.

MA Don't blame that on me.

DA   Can you not even trust your own!? And that little, blessed grandchild...

MA   Don't you dare...

DA   Curled safe, now, but what of the future?

MA   Don't you dare use that...

DA   I wanted something to pass on, to leave -

MA   Don't...

DA   An inheritance...

MA picks up a boning knife.

RORY   Missus...

MA   Don't you profane that child when you tried to kick it out of my daughter.

DA   Get back, Rory, she'll use it.

MA   I won't have you lying in my own hearing.

DA   Whatever you say, Breda. For the love of God, Rory, call someone, will you?

MA   Play your amateur dramatics. Oh yes, Rory, I'm mad, got BSE. Should be locked up. The old biddy's out-lived her usefulness, so just send her to the knackeryard. Funny, I thought that was my home. I'm amongst my own, here.

DA   She's raving. Call Skully.

MA   Or the police, that's what he'd like. But he can't, you see, because this business is about as bent as a copper coil. Cheap pheasants - they're poached.

DA   Whatever you say, Breda. Skedaddle, will you?

MA   And if the police come here, so would the health and safety inspectors, and then his empire would be no more.

DA   Whatever you say.

MA   Don't play-act with me. Pretending to shiver, a better story for the lad. "She was so wild, she even had the Bull man quaking". (*She puts down the knife*) I'm no more able to waste blood than you. You'd want Finoulla to turn it into black pudding so we could all eat your suffering. I won't eat and drink in remembrance of you.

She leaves.

DA		Rory lad, what was I after telling you? She's lost her head, she's a liability, she's - (*RORY leaves*) - Magnificent.

Scene Two

RORY on stage. FIN crosses, with a stool, which she puts in the large walk-in cold room. He watches her in silence. She exits, returning with a small folding table, which is also placed in the cold room. She exits. SKULLY enters, half-running, then pauses, as he is obviously not being pursued, as he thought. He looks off-stage, enters again at a half-run for a few paces. Stops. Looks mystified. Exits and enters several times. Stands, bemused.

SKULLY   There's something not right, here. This - (*he exits, half-enters*) - there's something missing...

RORY   The donkey.

SKULLY   Of course! I didn't have to duck or dive or run in, cupping the family jewels for fear of a -

RORY   - They came for her, as they warned. Brought a great padded van. Took her. like they said.

SKULLY   She - ?

RORY   - Fought them, just as I knew she would. Bit, scratched, kicked - did all she could to stop being put in that van.

SKULLY   When was this, son?

RORY   When you were supposed to be watching over her. They took her.

SKULLY   They?

RORY   The donkey sanctuary people. She's been liberated.

SKULLY   She was hardly held to hostage.

RORY   Liberated from a death camp, that's how they put it. Said it was cruel, her smelling blood all the time and hearing the screams of slaughter. The living conditions weren't much good, either.

SKULLY   It does us.

RORY   Said it was insanitary, unhygienic and inhumane.

SKULLY   So they're coming back for the rest of us, later? I fancy a big, well-built woman liberating me. Should I shave and pack a bag?

RORY   We don't count. We cause it. It's our own mess. We have choice.

SKULLY Ballox.

RORY Whereas a dumb creature doesn't, or so they said, ignoring her cries and screams and kicks. She didn't want to go. But they wouldn't give her that choice. They knew better.

SKULLY Jesus, isn't there a famine or a plague or a war somewhere to keep them occupied?

RORY That's not what they're interested in.

SKULLY Stealing a three legged donkey from a knackeryard's a sad state of affairs.

RORY And they were well planned. A midday swoop. They even wore balaclavas. One asked me if I was interested in joining the vegetarian society.

SKULLY I hope that's a joke.

RORY Aren't you sad? Do you not care? You were the one on look-out. If you'd been at your post they'd have never got in.

SKULLY I'm sorry about that, lad, but it's gone, now.

RORY It?

SKULLY She, he, it - the donkey. It's probably having the time of its life, now. Nice stable, green paddock, company. And you know what they say about being hung like a donkey... She's having the time of her life, she is. I could vouch for it. So put it all behind you, now. Here, have a tenner...

RORY You were in on it, weren't you?

SKULLY What?

RORY You let them in.

SKULLY Just take the money, lad, and we'll hear no more about it.

RORY You sold her.

SKULLY No! I - well - here... Here's a pony. I'll swap it for the donkey. Fair deal?

RORY And they had cameras, too. You knew about it. You betrayed us.

SKULLY Just take the fucking money. (*Thrusts money at RORY*)

RORY I wouldn't touch it.

SKULLY Don't be any more of a half-wit than you already are.

FIN enters, in white gown and rubber boots of the slaughterhouse, carrying rugs and blankets. She crosses to the cold room in silence. She is heavier in her pregnancy.

SKULLY For the love of Christ, take the money and get her some maternity clothes. Booties. A layette for the bab'. And look at the shocking state of them shoes. They're odd, not even a pair. Buy yourself some boots.

RORY I'd rather go barefoot.

SKULLY Where's your pride, boy?

RORY Dignity and principles are more important.

SKULLY Oh, hark at the big bold man, here, lecturing me. You've not tasted hunger, yet, lad. And when you do, you'll see only the wealthy can afford scruples. Only the middle-class have the wages to pay for dignity. Me, I'm not even working-class. I'm a scavenger and we have no loyalties except to ourselves. So wise-up, lad, for no fucker's gonna liberate you. This is it, ad infinitum, for the rest of your life. And the word on the street is, it'll get worse.

SKULLY leaves, throwing the money on the floor. FIN settled in the cold room on her stool with rugs, begins a lesson with RORY.

FIN Dismember, then re-member.

RORY Fin...

FIN Study.

 (*He approaches her, taking out a pad from his pocket and pencil from behind his ear*)

 With Beef, there's hocks -

RORY - The legs

FIN And the back side, which is -

RORY Silverside, topside, thick flank -

FIN   - Or 'bed'.

RORY   Aren't you cold?

FIN   The Fore-quarter...

RORY   Fin?

FIN   Chine, or -

RORY   - Thick rib.

FIN   And...

RORY   Brisket, Chuck and Plate.

FIN   I loved the words when I was a child. A strange continent, naming the parts. Hind-quarter...

RORY   Light flank, hipbone, sirloin. Aren't you cold?

FIN   In the cutting-room, watching him dismantle a pig into palm-sized bits. What's this? (*She touches her shoulder-blade*)

RORY   Chuck. The thick piece at the back of the shoulder. Fin?

FIN   And this? (*She touches her neck*)

RORY   Clod. Between the neck and the chuck. Will you come out?

FIN   It's clean in here. I fell in a pool of blood when I was a child. It soaked my knickers. There's no blood now. Dewlap...

RORY   Central chest of a beast. The loose skin from chin to brisket.

She approaches, guiding his hands to parts of her body.

FIN   And this?

RORY   The solar plexus.

FIN   In a beast?

RORY   Brisket.

FIN   This?

RORY   Leg. Shoulder. Neck. Loin.

FIN The four parts of lamb. And here?

RORY Sweetbread. The gland in a lamb's throat. *(He places his hand on her swollen belly)* And here?

FIN A stupid heifer in calf.

RORY Fin...

FIN There's nothing left, Rory, we're all but going under. You're our last chance, we're relying on you. So study, be prepared. I'd have entered the contest myself, but I can't get near the block. This bloody... *(She begins to make an action as though to punch herself in the stomach. Stops)* They don't let women enter, anyway. Whoever heard of a female master butcher? Or gutman...

RORY I want to make it all right.

FIN So don't forget your steel, oval knife, straight knife, tail grab -

RORY I want to make it all right for you and the -

FIN - Pole axe, cleaver, saw and your spreaders. Better bring the stun-gun as well, they may not want you to pole axe.

RORY Fin...

FIN Make sure your cow gown is clean. Spotless. And take the spare clogs - the wooden ones with leather uppers to the knee

RORY I love you

FIN We don't want them to think we're dirty. Be well turned out.

RORY Did you hear me?

FIN There's enough for them to bitch about us without giving them more ammunition on a plate.

RORY I want to make it all right.

FIN I.. How? How can you? How can you? How can you make it all right? Hhm? How? How? Tell me, how? How? How do you propose making things all right, ha? How? Tell me. Rory, tell me.

RORY I love you.

FIN Ha!

57

RORY	I want you.
FIN	Huh.
RORY	I want the baby.
FIN	Baby?
RORY	The baby.
FIN	What baby?
RORY	The... (*he points*)
FIN	Oh, you mean the little bastard.
RORY	Don't.
FIN	That's what my father calls it. That's its name. In later years, if it survives, it can say "My Grandfather named me. Yes, it seems to be an unusual name, but it's one that runs in the family. Mammy's 'bitch', Nanny's 'whore'..."
RORY	Stop it, stop it..
FIN	It's not yours, anyway.
RORY	God...
FIN	I'd like to be able to tell you what the father's name is, but I have no idea. His breath and his insistence... and engine oil tattooing his fingerprints... That's all I can tell you. It's not much, but it didn't take very long... just five minutes of hell up the back of an alley. He wasn't one for small talk, or introductions, or even consent..
RORY	Fin, I... (*He tries to be gentle, to embrace her*)
FIN	No. I want to go, now, where it's clean. And don't you dare pity me. Don't you dare...
RORY	I promise I'll make it all right. I swear. Oh, Fin, I -
FIN	It's too late.
RORY	Fin, it's never -
FIN	- It's too late.

She enters the fridge, closes the door. A beat. DA enters.

DA Books?! (*He raises RORY's notebook with diagrams of cuts*) Aw Jesus fucking Christ in heaven! It's studying books he's after doing, is it? (*He hits RORY at the back of the head. RORY does not respond*) What use would that be to a meat man? Studying. Books. It's the raw matter he should be getting his hands into. Books. What did a book ever tell you about precision killing? About the tip of the blade going into the neck? Are you paying attention? (*No response*) It's... instinctive. You have to have your hands on the warm clay. You feel the beast twitching beside you - feel the power of muscle beneath that lousy hide. The red triangle at the corner of the eye just before it gets an idea to buck, to give you a sideways kick. But no... You've got the upper hand... You're watching, feeling with it, breathing alongside until the moment when there's only one pair of lungs inflating and the beast has been transformed into something else. It's beautiful. I am the executioner, the Creator's opposite. What we do, Rory lad, is the mirror of Genesis. I take life and revert it to cold clay. I sculpt familiar objects from an obscure source. I -

RORY Teach me. I want to win.

Scene Three

SKULLY enters cautiously, in dapper clothes, carrying a knotted blanket full of his belongings. He notices the money on the ground and collects it. He tries to slink off as MA enters with RORY.

MA   It must be bad, then. Even the rats're jumping ship.

SKULLY   Ah, Breda. How's she cutting?

MA   Close to the jugular. And I have me boning knife handy.

SKULLY   Ah, you're a card.

MA   And you're the Joker. You can change suits. Heading back to the fancy one, are we? Had enough of our congenial hospitality? It's fine, but perhaps not by Knightsbridge standards. Wasn't the game well hung enough for you?

SKULLY   There's nothing like a bit of hanging to stretch and tenderize the muscles and tendons in a young pheasant.

MA   Ours have been hanging from the neck so long they've rotted and dropped off. And there's an awful lot of life in them, seeing they've been dead so long.

SKULLY   Ah, well..

MA   I almost believed it was Judgement Day, the dead rising up and walking, until I took a look at what it was that was crawling. No repentant sinners, there. Just corruption. So. Are you after following the donkey?

SKULLY   Trying to get it back, yes.

MA   I'd love to believe you, but I stopped having faith in fairytales a long time ago.

SKULLY   It's too jaded you've become. You're that jaundiced by life you paint everything in a poor light.

MA   Now that you mention it, you do have a greenish tinge about you. No - I believe it's more yellow - that cowardly, buttery sort of colour of a plucked chicken.

SKULLY   Now, Breda, I've always stood my round and held my corner.

MA   And you're not running out because we're finished?

SKULLY Finished? You and Bull? Never.

MA Because I'll give my last drop of blood before I quit here.

SKULLY Sure don't I know that?

MA And I'll stick the throat of anyone who dares to run out on me.

A beat.

SKULLY No, I was wrong, earlier. I should've kept the watch. I didn't, and I'm mightily sorry. The beast is gone because of me. It was my fault and now I'll try and rectify it.

MA By how?

SKULLY Getting the fekkin donkey back, if I can. If not, I'll buy one and amputate its leg.

MA Aren't you the clever, resourceful fella?

SKULLY I'm serious, Breda. It'll slay him, it will, his doaty gone.

MA Good. It'll be doing me a favour.

SKULLY Jesus, woman, have you no warmth or love in you at all?

MA Have you?

Hear DA, off, talking to the donkey, as usual. No braying.

DA Aw, yes, my sugar, I'll pole-axe you... I'll... (*He enters*) Where's my little beast gone?

SKULLY It's red sorrow will be on me today if he takes the news bad.

MA It'll make a change from the black sorrow I spend my life in. Well, go on. You can break it to him. Your tongue is honey-coated, so I'm told.

DA Where is she? She never come running to greet me, as she normally does.

MA To head-butt him and try out her teeth on his dewlap.

DA It's the school again, isn't it? They have her loaned for the nativity play.

MA She ran amok in the hall last year. Broke three windows, terrified fifty

	infants with tea-cloths on their heads and tried to mount the headmaster.
DA	Isn't she a great little beast, altogether? (*He exits, looking*)
SKULLY	He likes them vicious, like his women.

(*RORY exits, following DA*)

	Will you not tell him, Breda? Let me slip off and try to recapture her? Be kind, put on a soft face..
MA	Where have you been these thirty years? I'd no more do that than let the creditors take the yard. They'd have to burn me out, first.
SKULLY	But he'll take it that bad...
MA	If you're not ready to cut the head of him, you're up to your neck in the blood vat for love of him, next.
SKULLY	Blood is thicker than water.
MA	And it congeals and clots and grows sluggish. It runs the quicker when water's added and I'd add a pint, quickly, if I were you. If you were any more stationary you'd be six feet under. What is it? Fear? Or has the little tick swallowed its fill?

DA enters with RORY.

DA	Breda! Skully! The fucking, bastardising lot. They have my sweetheart taken! Where's my flaying knife? I'll skin them, I will, I'll hoist them up on the beef tree and saw them in two.

The fridge door opens, revealing FIN.

MA	Mary, Mother of God.
FIN	When sticking a beast, you cut the jugular vein where it crosses over the bottom of the throat, just before the brisket.

RORY approaches FIN.

RORY	The brisket is the solar plexus... the thick part of the breast between the rib bones.
MA	Look at the state of her with your meat lessons and junket.
DA	Sssh... She's teaching him.

FIN   You cut in, behind the windpipe...

RORY   ... But if you cut too deep, the blood will run back, staining the ribcage.

DA   He has it right. You go on, Rory boy.

SKULLY slips away.

FIN   The meat is overstuck when this happens.

MA   Finoulla?

FIN   It won't do any harm..

RORY   ... it's just not good butchering.

DA   Well said, lad!

MA   Finoulla, stop this right now.

DA   Leave them!

FIN   You can't overstick lamb..

RORY   ... as lamb is stuck behind the ear at the jugular.

MA   Finoulla!

DA catches MA as she approaches FIN.

DA   Do you want to lose this business?

FIN   I think I'm overstuck, Rory.

DA   Well? (*MA steps back from him but listens*)

FIN   The blood seeps in, behind my ribcage.

DA   I tell you Breda, he's better than we ever thought. We have a chance yet with the competition, but you have to leave them be.

MA   Enough chance to save the yard?

DA   If they're running a book and the odds are high...

FIN   Will it be alright, Rory?

RORY   It will. I'll make everything alright.

DA   We'll teach the fuckers to try and over-run us! Teach them a lesson they won't forget!

FIN   I'm over-stuck, Rory. The blades gone in too deep behind the windpipe.

DA   And we'll conquer, we'll over-rule.

MA   I hate you.

DA   But you're with me. Together, we'll over-rule.

FIN   I'm stained, Rory.

RORY   (*To DA*) It was Skully betrayed us.

Scene Four

SKULLY is shackled on a long chain to a pulley, the winch used for the beef tree. There is evidence on his face and by his clothes he has been beaten. MA enters, removing the striped apron for front of shop.

MA Oh well, that's it, then. (*She tidies the already clean block*)

SKULLY Shouldn't you be in the front of shop? With the lad at the competition and the Bull playing coach, you're making it desperate easy for a scallion to make off with your debts.

MA If I offered free sirloin with every purchase, I still wouldn't have a customer. I have the shop open and unattended and the only thing going through the door is the woodcock, crawling to join its pals in the gutter.

SKULLY It's bad, then?

MA Not only were we in the documentary the other night, we've made the papers for the fourth day running.

SKULLY Are we quoted?

MA Ah, yes - there's a choice quote from your brother with that many asterisks, I was seeing stars.

SKULLY Photos?

MA Some.

SKULLY Of me? Did they get my good side?

MA The one with or without the bruises?

SKULLY I've been told I have an aquiline, noble nose.

MA Well your best feature is banjaxed now the Bull has it broken. As to the photos, they weren't from here. The first lot, from the handbills your mates used when picketing the shop, were us, no mistake. But the ones, now... they're from some battlefield.

SKULLY And no sign of our side of the story?

MA Conscientious butchering doesn't sell. Still, at least it's that biased, you can tell.

SKULLY Us, maybe, but not the customers.

MA   Fek them. It's all down to Rory, now. If he can make it to the finals, maybe that'll salvage our reputation. The Master Butcher of the year in Slaughterhouse Bloodbath doesn't quite ring true. It'll save our name, if nothing else.

A beat.

SKULLY   Breda, now the place is quiet and we have it to ourselves, are you on for it?

MA   For what?

SKULLY   A shag. The old in-out.

MA   Well it's certainly more direct, but I think I preferred the poetic approach.

SKULLY   Blunt prose is more suited to these conditions. D'you want it, then, or not?

MA   Not.

SKULLY   C'mon, Breda, a quickie, here, on the block. For me, a little Christmas fuck.

MA   I've had enough of bondage what with being tied in marriage to a man I loathe, without coupling in chains with his brother.

SKULLY   C'mon Breda, it's your best offer yet. And let's face it, probably your last. You're not getting any younger.

MA   Nor you any more attractive.

SKULLY   You're a knacker; finished. It's as well you're here.

MA   I thought, once, you were a tick, jumping from body to body, taking your fill from wherever your fancy led you. I see, now, you're not so discerning. A maggot it is you are. Wherever there's shit and rotting flesh, so there will be you. You're happiest, then.

SKULLY   Tell me, Breda, do children scream and run from you when you walk down the street?

MA   I think them chains must be on very tight. They're constricting the flow of blood to the brain. (*She starts steeling a knife. A beat*) The things they said went on in here... Unnecessary cruelty in the killing, no water in the death pens. D'you know, they even said we gelded without compassion. (*She takes out calves' testes and begins cutting them*) Just castrated with a smile on our face. Can you imagine that? Didn't use the gelding rings, letting nature take its course. Just chained them up and... (*She chops once with her cleaver*) That's that.

Silence. She continues cutting. Several beats. DA enters from front of shop, draped in Christmas decorations. He begins to hang glitter boas on the meat rails.

DA　　Hang them up! Celebrate! The fuckin' little beauty... He's through he is, into the grand slam!

MA　　Did you put the money on him, like we said?

DA　　I did. 100-1 to win, he was, when I got the tote. He's evens, now. The little scutty darlin'... I could squeeze him to death, I could.

(*FIN enters*)

You should have seen him... dazzling, he was, his overalls that white... a light seemed to shine from him, and for all the attention they paid, you'd think he was the only one in the cutting room. Oh, he learnt from me, alright. The image of me when I starting out and as gentle as could be, asking pardon of the chicken before he poked its parson's nose. He did! The little fekkin' tinker; it was as if he knew the judges would be looking for personality as well as beauty of execution.

MA　　How did he go with the other rounds?

DA　　He won Dressing of a Chicken on artistic merit alone and Portioning of a Pig was an act of technical brilliance! Breda, the way he snuck the blade in round the ball and socket joint - with a pause, the tiniest frown to make us think it had him beaten and then a parry with his boning knife and he had it off, clean as a whistle. The performance was inspired, and he won the Charismatic Boning-out Commendation, to boot. I tell yous, there's none can hold a fucking cleaver to him.

MA　　So...?

DA　　It's just the last round, now: Precision Killing.

SKULLY　And won't he win it, sure, there's no competition with you as the..

DA notices SKULLY, approaches. SKULLY shrinks.

DA　　Well?

SKULLY　Oh, Bull, I was -

DA — Well? (*A beat. He rattles the chains*) Come on, boy, I'm expecting something..

SKULLY Bull, I -

DA Come on!

SKULLY Not before the women..

DA Don't let me down, now...

SKULLY I will but, Bull please, don't make me in public.

DA There's something you've got to do for me...

SKULLY I know, I... please..

DA So...?

SKULLY I... I'm... D'you remember when we were children and the way we ran wild in the fields and Mammy's despair of us and her saying we'd send her to an early grave...

DA I'm waiting...

SKULLY ... And the shenanigans we'd get up to and the laughs! Jesus, the craic! And you called me your left hand man and I was there for you and how Dado bet us so hard when we cut the girls' long hair when them asleep and we stole the butter to put on our arses to cool them down, but instead they cooked and we roared and bawled so much Mammy thought the cow had slipped her calf and come running out to us and her melting at the sight of us and kissing us and giving comfort...

FIN Da...

DA I'm getting impatient.

SKULLY and how she made us swear to be friends forever and I was, I did...

FIN Da...

SKULLY ... That time you shat on the teacher's desk and him knowing it was you but he couldn't take the belt to you without proof and him twisting my ear to make me blub but I wouldn't, I didn't,

FIN Daddy..

DA Traitors have to be punished.

SKULLY   and him fierce because he wanted to tan you but he couldn't so he bet me and I crying as the switch come down and him saying denounce him, denounce the devil and I know he meant you but I wouldn't, you were my brother and they made me wait a year for holy communion and it was a sin and a shame but I wouldn't denounce you,

FIN   Please, Da

DA   Hold that tongue, girl.

SKULLY   and Mammy crying then giving me the silent treatment and she stopped hugging and tucking me in at night and would never come, no matter how loud I called her and we grew up then, big boys overnight and you said we were outlaws and we'd show them, yes, we'd show the fekkin world with me with the gab and you with the swagger and we'd never let them see us cry

DA   I want to hear you..

SKULLY   so don't make me do it now, for the love of God, Bull, give me some decency, give me some charity, give me some

DA   I want to hear you bray.

SKULLY   respect. Haven't you me beaten enough? Don't take away the one thing

DA   I want to hear you hee-haw

SKULLY   I have, my humanness, my self-respect, my words

DA   Hee-haw, come on, donkey, hee-haw

SKULLY   Please Bull

DA   Hee-haw

FIN   Daddy -

DA   Hee-haw

SKULLY   Leave me with my words, take anything else, leave me with my words

FIN moves forward to help, MA restrains her.

MA   Don't be a fekkin eejit, let him do it.

FIN   Da... stop...

MA   Let him soil his bed; let the world see him for what he is.

SKULLY Bull... Hee-haw

DA   Louder.

SKULLY Hee-haw...

FIN   Don't...

DA   Again.

SKULLY Hee-haw, hee-haw, hee-haw (*he is broken*)

DA   That's it, my sugar

SKULLY Hee-haw, hee-haw, hee-haw

DA   My sweetheart, I'll put a bullet in your brain one day and then you'll be sorry.

FIN breaks from them all and leaves to the cold room.

Scene Five

MA enters. FIN is sitting by the open door to the cold room, SKULLY still chained. FIN ignores MA; SKULLY is vacantly humming.

MA Well, it's my belief the calves have the scour, the sow's down with bonnives and the cows have foot and mouth. (*A beat*) Any news? (*Silence*) Were them carol singers back? I thought I heard something. Still, they'd have to be real martyrs to return after your father took after them with the cattle prod. I swear, some hit high notes that'll never be reached again. And that was just the bass. There's nothing like that electric sting - Ha? (*Silence*) I found what was blocking the toilet. (*She throws down a wet pigeon*) It's bad enough a bird in the house, let alone one drowned in your own piss. (*A beat*) Anyone try to get in? I said: Anyone try to -

FIN No.

MA Oh, so it does talk. I was half expecting a party in full swing: The Animal Libbers, Health and Safety, the bailiffs and creditors - not forgetting the photographers and reporters - all jivin' along to the latest release from Mumbling Jesus, there, in the corner. (*She indicates SKULLY*) Has he said anything?

(*Silence but for his mumbling*)

Skully? Oi! Old Rag and Bones in the corner there! Where's the flightless wings of poesy gone? Skully?

(*She enters into dialogue, playing both Skully and herself*)

(*'Doing' SKULLY*) "Aw, Breda, it's a dying-out fire you've become." And I suppose you're a raging furnace? "You're not Phoebus the sun, but a tray of ashes and burnt-out cinders. You need a good poke to get the warmth going again and I know just the fella to do it." It's no hardship for me to be without your banter. I can play it myself; my very own little ventriloquist act. I don't need yous. Neither of yous are irreplaceable. But it was him did it to me. Just remember that.

She exits. FIN approaches SKULLY who is rattling old rosary beads.

FIN Skully? Can you hear me?

SKULLY (*Barely audible*) And k-cuf the l-rigs, Mother of God, pray for us sinners (*He laughs*)

FIN Uncle Skully...?

SKULLY   Kool the gels on the l-rig, eh, Llub? Now at the rouh of our

FIN   One day it'll be all over.

SKULLY   Death nema. Hail yram, lluf of grace, eht l-rigs are flighty little birds,

FIN   Skully?

SKULLY   desselb art thou amongst l-rigs, the little cuntin

He continues mumbling, low, as FIN moves away. A beat.

FIN   When I was little, I fell again and again on the same knee. The crust of the scab would never heal. It would be cracked or picked off. I did it myself, with a perverse pleasure in scarring, leaving a track, a trail, a sign that would never mend. That pink crinkled flesh. Tender. Not yet born. But I grew out of it.

Several beats. DA enters, howling and rending his clothing. MA enters, hearing the noise.

DA   Jesus, Mary and all the fucking saints in heaven! I'll weep, I will, a grown man slain!

MA   What is it?

DA   Ah, they're scalding, scalding, tears - they'll finish me, they will, I'll be away in me box.

MA   What?!

DA   Finoulla, be sure to bury me with my doaty - and not cremation - no, not the fire. I suffered enough with the flames when I alive. Burning, burning I am..

MA   What in God's name...?

DA   (*Suddenly calm*) It's over.

MA   The competition? How did..

DA   ...The dream. The whole, fucking, slagging lot.

FIN   Where's Rory?

MA   What happened? How did the finals...

DA	We're ruined. It's all gone. Everything.
FIN	Where's Rory?
DA	Skully, Finoulla - what'll we do? It's all over.
MA	It'll never be over.
FIN	Where's Rory?
DA	A hundred to fucking one. I had it all, everything, resting on that bet. It was a dead cert. All but home and dry.
FIN	Rory - ?
DA	He had class. Nothing could stop him. But they didn't give him a beast. Not beef. Not pork. A fucking sheep. He had it cut and open before he saw it was in lamb. Wouldn't continue. In lamb. He withdrew, in tears over a bastard fucking ewe. A hundred to fucking one.
DA	And gone. Over a... You. It's you that's done this. *(He approaches MA)* I should put a ring of skulls at your feet, you fuckin' knacker. You with your evil eye. You've cursed me from the start.
MA	Ah, yes, it's always me. It was me suggested you invest all we have in rotting game, was it?
FIN	Mam...
MA	Compete by taking on the quality... Since when did they come slumming it down here? Was it me who sold the frigging donkey and brought the trouble down on our heads?
DA	She was a grand little beast.
MA	And who got rid of her?
FIN	No...
MA	If it wasn't for a certain person and his high falutin' ideas, she'd still be here braying and kicking for all her worth.
DA	You!

DA rushes towards SKULLY and begins to hoist him up on the winch. SKULLY's mumbled nonsensical prayers get louder, more urgent.

SKULLY For thine is the kingdom, eht rewop and eht yrolg... Mary, Mother of God!

FIN Put him down!

DA That's the best thing for him. You put down useless beasts.

He begins to hoist him onto the beef tree.

SKULLY Pray for me. Oh Jesus, sweet Jesus...

DA That'll teach you.

MA stops FIN from leaving and getting help.

MA You can't run with the fox and hunt with the hounds.

DA places SKULLY on the beef tree, in an inverted crucifix.

DA Anyone not with me is against me. Ha, Breda?

SKULLY Jesus...

FIN No! (*She breaks away*)

MA No decency. No care. He thinks more about a three legged donkey than the rest of us put together.

SKULLY Mary, blessed virgin -

DA What did I say about words, ass?

SKULLY intercede for me..

MA I may look like my heart's been pierced by swords, but you've got the wrong martyred mother.

FIN Have you no shame?

MA Only people without history have nothing to be ashamed of.

FIN I will never be like you. (*She goes towards the beef tree*)

DA I'll warn you once, girl. (*FIN moves toward the block*) It's all gone.

FIN Good.